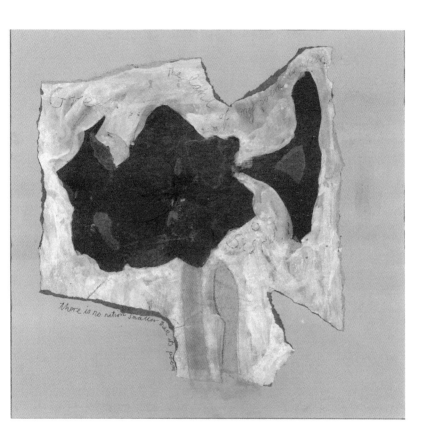

there is no nation smaller than the poem

green

the shape of my poem

it grows

the song

remember her

as she was

from past to past

fertile

and

I have of her

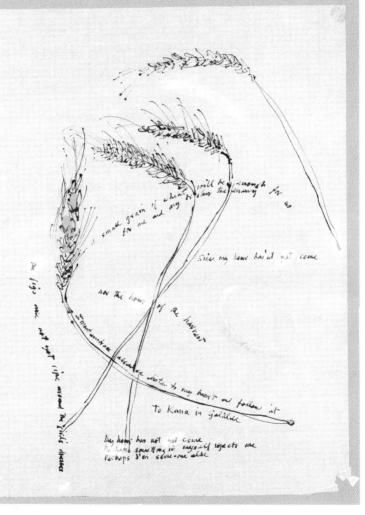

a small grain of wheat will be enough for us
for me and my brother to share the journey

since my hour has'nt yet come

on the hour of the harvest

I must continue elsewhere listen to my heart and follow it

to Kana in galilee

my hour has not not come
Perhaps something in myself rejects me
Perhaps I'm someone else

the legs once not yet ripe around the fields shelter

green
the land of my poem is green
the song
carries
(Non past)
fertile
her was
to past

And I have of her:

And I have of her

And I have of her
what is common in the sayings

prophets

Narcissus contemplating the waters of his image

The sharpness of shadows in symmetry and the exactitude of meaning

on the roof of the night

The donkey of wisdom abandoned mocking his dreams and her reality

And I have of her on a hill

And I have of her

And I have of her

The symbols stuffed with memories opposites

Realism doesn't find

Abstraction doesn't lead to illuminations

my other self I have of her
Singers can only inscribe her days in a diary
If the dream isn't enough
I'll be heroically sleepless at the door of exile
And I have of her: The echo of my language from the walls
removing salt from the sea
At the very moment when my strong heart betrays me

Mural

Mural

Mahmoud Darwish

Translated by
Rema Hammami and John Berger

With an Introduction by
John Berger

VERSO
London • New York

This paperback edition first published by Verso 2017
First published by Verso 2009
© Estate of Mahmoud Darwish 2009, 2017
Translation © Rema Hammami and John Berger
Introduction © John Berger

1 3 5 7 9 10 8 6 4 2

Verso
UK: 6 Meard Street, London W1F 0EG
US: 20 Jay Street, Suite 1010, Brooklyn, NY 11201
versobooks.com

Verso is the imprint of New Left Books

ISBN-13: 978-1-78663-057-5
ISBN-13: 978-1-78663-058-2 (UK EBK)
ISBN-13: 978-1-78663-059-9 (US EBK)

British Library Cataloguing in Publication Data
A catalogue record for this book is available from the British Library

Library of Congress Cataloging-in-Publication Data
A catalog record for this book is available from the Library of Congress

Typeset in Garamond by Hewer Text UK Ltd, Edinburgh

Printed and bound by CPI Group (UK) Ltd, Croydon, CR0 4YY

To Mahmoud, with thanks for his generous encouragement

We would like to thank Maria Nadotti, Tania Nazir, Leila Chahid, Alex Pollock and Beverly Bancroft for making this collaboration possible.

R.H. and J.B.

Contents

Al Rabweh

by John Berger

A few days after our return from what was thought of, until recently, as the future state of Palestine, and which is now the world's largest prison (Gaza) and the world's largest waiting room (the West Bank), I had a dream.

I was alone, standing, stripped to the waist, in a sandstone desert. Eventually somebody else's hand scooped up some dusty soil from the ground and threw it at my chest. It was a considerate rather than an aggressive act. The soil or gravel changed, before it touched me, into torn strips of cloth, probably cotton, which wrapped themselves around my torso. Then these tattered rags changed again and became words, phrases. Written not by me but by the place.

Remembering this dream, the invented word <u>landswept</u> came to my mind. Repeatedly. Landswept describes a place or places where everything, both material and immaterial, has been brushed aside, purloined, swept away, blown down, irrigated off, everything except the touchable earth.

There's a small hill called Al Rabweh on the western outskirts of Ramallah, it's at the end of Tokyo street. Near the top of this hill the poet Mahmoud Darwish is buried. It's not a cemetery.

The street is named Tokyo because it leads to the city's Cultural Centre, which is at the foot of the hill, and was built thanks to Japanese funding.

It was in this Centre that Darwish read some of his poems for the last time – though no one then supposed it would be the last. What does the word *last* mean in moments of desolation?

We went to visit the grave. There's a headstone. The dug earth is still bare, and mourners have left on it little sheaves of green wheat – as he suggested in one of his poems. There are also red anemones, scraps of paper, photos.

He wanted to be buried in Galilee where he was born and where his mother still lives, but the Israelis forbade it.

At the funeral tens of thousands of people assembled here, at Al Rabweh. His mother, 96 years old, addressed them. "He is the son of you all," she said.

In exactly what arena do we speak when we speak of loved ones who have just died or been killed? Our words seem to us to resonate in a present moment more present than those we normally live. Comparable with moments of making love, of facing imminent danger, of taking an irrevocable decision, of dancing a tango. It's not in the arena of the eternal that our words of mourning resonate, but it could be that they are in some small gallery of that arena.

On the now deserted hill I tried to recall Darwish's voice. He had the calm voice of a beekeeper:

A box of stone
where the living and dead move in the dry clay
like bees captive in a honeycomb in a hive
and each time the siege tightens
they go on a flower hunger strike
and ask the sea to indicate the emergency exit.

Recalling his voice, I felt the need to sit down on the touchable earth, on the green grass. I did so.

Al Rabweh means in Arabic: "the hill with green grass on it". His words have returned to where they came from. And there is nothing else. A nothing shared by 5 million people.

The next hill, 500 metres away, is a refuse dump. Crows are circling it. Some kids are scavenging.

When I sat down in the grass by the edge of his newly dug grave, something unexpected happened. To define it, I have to describe another event.

This was a few days ago. My son, Yves, was driving and we were on our way to the local town of Cluses in the French Alps. It had been snowing. Hillsides, fields and trees were white and the whiteness of the first snow often disorientates birds, disturbing their sense of distance and direction.

Suddenly a bird struck the windscreen. Yves, watching it in the rear-mirror, saw it fall to the roadside. He braked and reversed. It was a small bird, a robin, stunned but still alive, eyes blinking. I picked him up out of the snow, he was warm in my hand, very warm and we drove on.

From time to time I examined him. Within half an hour he had died. I lifted him up to put him on the back seat of the car. Yes, he was a male. What surprised me was his weight. He weighed less than when I had picked him up from the snow. I moved him from hand to hand to check this. It was as if his energy when alive, his struggle to survive, had added to his weight. He was now almost weightless.

After I sat on the grass on the hill of Al Rabweh something comparable happened. Mahmoud's death had lost its weight. What had remained were his words.

Months have passed, each one filled with foreboding and silence. Disasters are flowing together into a delta that has no name, and will only be given one by geographers, who will come later, much later. Nothing to do today but to try to walk on the bitter waters of this nameless delta.

Gaza, the largest prison in the world, is being transformed into an abattoir. The word *strip* (from Gaza Strip) is being drenched with blood, as happened 65 years ago to the word *ghetto*.

Day and night bombs, shells, phosphorous arms, mortars, machine-gun rounds are being fired by the Israeli army from air, sea and land against a civilian population of 1.5 million. The estimated number of mutilated and dead increases with each news report from international journalists, all of whom are forbidden by Israel to enter the Strip. Yet the crucial constant figure is that for a single Israeli casualty there are one hundred Palestinian casualties, of whom almost half are women and children. This is what constitutes a massacre. Most lodgings have neither water nor electricity; the hospitals lack doctors, medicines and generators. The massacre follows a blockage and siege.

Certain voices across the world are raised in protest. But the governments of the rich, with their world media and their proud possession of nuclear weapons, reassure Israel that a blind eye will be cast on what its soldiers are perpetrating.

"A place weeping enters our sleep," wrote the Kurdish poet Bejan Matur, "a place weeping enters our sleep and never leaves."

Nothing but landswept earth.

I am back, four months ago in Ramallah, in an abandoned underground parking lot, which has been taken over as a working-space by a small group of Palestinian painters and sculptors, amongst whom there's a sculptress named Randa Mdah. I'm looking at an installation conceived and made by her entitled Puppet Theatre.

It consists of a large bas-relief measuring 3 metres by 2, which stands upright like a wall. In front of it on the floor there are three fully sculptured figures.

The bas-relief of shoulders, faces, hands, is made on an armature of wire, of polyester, fibreglass and clay. Its surfaces are coloured – darkish greens, browns, reds. The depth of its relief is about the same as in one of Ghiberti's bronze doors for the Duomo in Firenze, and the foreshortening and distorted perspectives have been dealt with with almost the same mastery. (I would never have guessed that the artist is so young. She's 26.) The wall of the bas-relief, in its crowdedness and with its ceremonial colours, is like "the hedge" that an audience in a theatre resembles when seen from the stage.

On the floor in front are the life-size figures, two women and one man. They are made of the same materials, but with more faded colours.

One is within touching distance of the audience, another is two metres away and the third twice as far away again. They are wearing their everyday clothes, the ones they chose to put on this morning.

Their bodies are attached to cords hanging from three horizontal sticks which in turn hang from the ceiling. They are the puppets, their sticks the control bars for the absent, or invisible puppeteers.

The multitude of figures on the bas-relief are all looking at what they see in front of their eyes and wringing their hands. Their hands are like flocks of poultry.

They are wringing them because they are powerless to intervene. They are bas-relief, they are not three-dimensional, and so they cannot enter or intervene in the solid real world.

Some of them look like commentators, some look like angels, some look like government spokesmen, some look like Presidents, some look like fiends. All express impotency. Together and collectively, despite their wringing hands, they represent silence.

The three solid, palpitating figures attached to the invisible puppeteers' cords, are being hurled to the ground, head first, feet in the air. Again and again until their heads split. Their hands, torsos, faces are convulsed in agony. One that doesn't reach its end. You see it in their feet. Again and again.

I could walk between the impotent spectators of the bas-relief and the sprawling victims on the ground. But I don't. There is a power in this work such as I have rarely seen. It has claimed the very ground on which it is standing. It has made the killing field between the unreal spectators and the agonising victims sacred. It has changed the floor of a parking lot into something landswept.

This unforgettable work prophesied the Gaza Strip.

Mahmoud Darwish's grave on the hill of Al Rabweh has now, following decisions made by the Palestinian Authority, been fenced off, and a glass pyramid has been constructed over it. It's no longer possible to squat beside him. His words, however, are audible to our ears and will remain so and we can repeat them.

I have work to do on the geography of volcanoes
From desolation to ruin
from the time of Lot to Hiroshima
As if I'd never yet lived
with a lust I've still to know
Perhaps Now has gone further away
and yesterday come closer
So I take Now's hand to walk along the hem of history
and avoid cyclic time
with its chaos of mountain goats
How can my tomorrow be saved?
By the velocity of electronic time

or by my desert caravan slowness?
I have work till my end
as if I won't see tomorrow
and I have work for today who isn't here
So I listen
softly softly
to the ant beat of my heart . . .

Ramallah and Haute Savoie
Early autumn, 2008

Mural

Here is your name
said the woman
and vanished in the corridor

A hand's reach away I see heaven
a dove's white wing transporting me to another childhood
and I don't dream that I'm dreaming
Everything is real
I meet myself at my side
And fly

I will become what will be in the final circuit
Everything is white
The sea hanging above a roof of white clouds
in the sky of the absolute white nothingness
I was and was not
Here alone at the white frontier of eternity.

I came before my hour so no angel approaches to ask:
what did you do over there in the world?

I don't hear the chorus of the righteous or wailing of
    sinners
I'm alone in whiteness
alone . . .

At the gate of resurrection nothing hurts
neither time past nor any feeling
I don't sense the lightness of things nor the weight of
    apprehension
There's no one to ask:
where now is my where?
Where is the city of death
Where am I?
In this no-here . . .
no-time
and nothingness

As if I had died already
I know this story
I know that I go towards what I don't know
Perhaps I'm still alive somewhere
Aware of what I want . . .

One day I'll become what I want
One day I will become a thought
that no sword or book can dispatch to the wasteland
A thought equal to rain on the mountain split open by a
    blade of grass
where power will not triumph
and justice is not fugitive

One day I'll become what I want
One day I'll become a bird
that plucks my being from nothingness.
As my wings burn I approach the truth
and rise from the ashes
I am the dialogue of dreamers
I shunned body and self to complete the first journey
    towards meaning
but it consumed me then vanished
I am that absence
The fugitive from heaven

One day I'll become what I want
One day I'll become a poet
Water obedient to my vision
My language a metaphor for metaphors
I don't speak or indicate a place
Place is my sin and subterfuge
I am from there
My here leaps from my footstep to my imagination . . .
I am from what was or will be
I was created and destroyed in the expanse of the endless
    void

One day I'll become what I want
One day I'll become a vine
Let summer distil from me now
so passers-by beneath the chandeliers of this most sugared
    place
may drink my wine!

I am the message and the messenger
The small addresses and the post

One day I'll become what I want

Here is your name
said the woman
and vanished in the corridor of her whiteness
Here is your name, memorize it well!
Don't quibble over a letter of the alphabet
Ignore the tribal banners
Be friendly to your name which doesn't stand but lies
    across the page
Test it out with the living and the dead
Train it in its proper pronunciation with strangers
Write it on a rock in the empty cave
O my name: you will grow as I do
You will carry me as I carry you
for strangers are brothers to strangers
We'll entice the feminine with a vowel devoted to flutes
Oh my name: where are we now?
Speak out: what is now what is tomorrow?
What is time and place?
What's old what's new?

One day we'll become what we want
The journey hasn't begun and the path hasn't ended
The wise haven't reached their exile
nor the exiles their wisdom
The only flower we know is the red anemone

Come let's go towards the highest mural:
The land of my poem is green and high
God's words at dawn are the land of my poem
and I'm the faraway
far away

In every breeze a woman mocks her poet:
Collect the woman you saw in me
who was shattered
and give me back my femininity
for I have nothing left to do but contemplate the lake's
    wrinkles
Get rid of my tomorrow
Return my yesterday
and leave us alone together
After you
nothing leaves and nothing returns

Take back the poem if you want
for me there's only you in it
Take back your "I"
The exile will be complete with what's left of handwriting
    written for the carrier pigeons
At the end which me am I in us?
Of the two of us
let me be the last
A star will fall between the written and the said
A memory will lay out its thoughts: we were born in the
    time of the sword and the trumpet
between the fig and the cactus

Death was slower then more clear there was a truce across
   the mouth of the river
Now the electronic button works alone
the killer doesn't hear his victims
and the martyrs don't read out a testament

What breeze brought you here?
Tell me the name of your wound and I'll tell you the road
   where we'll lose ourselves twice!
Your heartbeats hurt me for they lead to the time of legends
My blood hurts me
Salt hurts me . . .
and my jugular vein

In the broken jug the women of the Syrian plains lament
   the length of the journey
and are scorched by the August sun
I saw them on the road to the well before my birth
and I heard the water in the clay weeping for them:
Return to the clouds and bring the carefree days

An echo said:
Nothing returns save the mighty past of the strong on
   their obelisks . . .
their traces in gold
and the prayers of the weak addressed to tomorrow
Give us our daily bread
and a stronger now
for there's neither reincarnation nor home nor eternity for us

An echo said:
I'm fed up with my incurable hope
sick of aesthetic traps: what is there after Babel?
The more the road clears to heaven
and the unknown reveals a final goal
the more the prose becomes prayer-like
and the song shatters

Green
The land of my poem is green and high
coming to me from the bed of my precipice
Strange you are
It's enough that you alone are there
to become a tribe ...
I sang in order to feel the wasted horizon in the pain of a
    dove
not to explain what God says to man
I'm no prophet
I don't proclaim that my fall is an ascent

I am the stranger from all I was given by my language
And if I've given my affections to Arabic
They have surrendered me to the feminine participle
And the words when far
are a land bordering a distant star
And the words when near
are an exile
And writing is not enough for me to declare:
I found my presence filling in absence
and whenever I searched for myself I found others

and whenever I searched for them I found only myself
the stranger
Am I a crowd of one?

I am the stranger
Obliged to cross the Milky Way seeking the beloved
Condemned by his gifts
that ruin appearances
The form shrinks the words get bigger
and go beyond the needs of my vocabulary
And in mirrors I look at myself:
Am I him?
Did I perform my role well in the last act?
Did I read the play before the performance?
or was it imposed on me?
Am I a performer?
or the dupe who changed the lines to live the post-modern
when the writer deserts his text and both actor and
        audience leave?

I sit behind the door and watch:
Am I him?
It's my language
Its voice has the sting of my blood
but the author is someone else
I am not me if I come and don't arrive
if I speak and don't utter
I am the one to whom dark letters say:
Write to be!
Read to discover!

And if you wish to speak do so
with your opposites united in meaning . . .
and your transparent self the main verse

I am surrounded by mariners with no port
A squall has bereft me of verbs and signs
I haven't had time to establish my exact position
I haven't asked about the strange resemblance of the two
    doors
Exit and Entrance
and I can't find a corpse to hunt for life
or a voice to shout:
O time in a hurry!
You kidnapped me with the words of a dark alphabet:
the real is the only sure thing imagined

O time that won't wait . . .
Won't wait for one who was late for his birth
Make from the past the only thing you say to us,
Your future
Like it was when we were friends
and not the victims of your chariot
without leading it without being led by it

I have seen what the dead remember and forget . . .
They don't grow up
They know what time it is by their wrist watches
And don't give a damn for our death or their lives
for what I was or will be
With them everything dissolves

He into me I into you
There's neither whole nor parts
No one living says to the dead: be me!
... elements like feelings dissolve
But I don't see my body there
I'm in neither the fullness of my death
nor the fullness of my first life
As if I'm not made of me
Who am I?
The deceased or the newborn?

Time is at zero
I wasn't thinking of birth when death carried me into chaos
I was neither living nor dead
And there is no nothingness or being

My nurse says: you are better now
And injects me with a tranquilizer:
Be calm
and worthy of what you're about to dream
even a little ...

I saw my French doctor
open my prison cell
and beat me with a stick
assisting him were two local policemen

I saw my father return
from the Hajj
fainted from the Hijazi sunstroke

he said to the flock of angels surrounding him:
Extinguish me!

I saw Moroccan boys playing soccer
pelting me with stones:
Pass your word back and scram!
and leave us our mother
O father trespassing in the cemetery!

I saw Rene Char
sitting with Heidegger
two metres away from me
I saw them drinking wine
not looking for poetry
The dialogue was a ray of light
And there was a passer-by waiting

I saw three comrades weeping
as they were sewing me a shroud
with gold thread

I saw Ma'ari expel his critics
from his poem
I'm not blind
To see what you all see
Vision is a light that leads to nothingness . . . or madness

I saw countries embrace my good mornings saying:
Be worthy of the bread's aroma
May the flowers of the pavement make you elegant

There's still fire on your mother's hearth
And the welcome is as warm as bread!

Green
The land of my poem is green
One stream is enough to make me whisper to the
    butterfly:
O sister
One stream is enough to solder the ancient myths
    onto the falcon's wing as it swaps banners for distant
    peaks
there where armies have founded for me a kingdom of
    oblivion
There is no nation smaller than its poem
But weapons make words too big for the living
and the dead who inhabit the living
And letters make the sword on the dawn's belt glitter
til the desert becomes parched for songs or drowns in
    them

No life is long enough for me to join my end to my
    beginning
The shepherds took my story and hid it in the grass
covering the magic debris where the tents once stood
and like this with trumpets and choral rhymes they
    cheated oblivion
then left me the hoarseness of memory on the stone of
    farewell
And they didn't return . . .

Pastoral our days are pastoral between city and tribe
I can't find a secret night for your saddle studded with
    mirages
You said to me: without you why do I need a name?
Call me
for I created you when you named me
and you killed me once you owned the name
How could you kill me?
Me the outcast of all this night
Let me enter the forest of your desire
Embrace me, hold me, squeeze me til
I shed pure nuptial honey on the hive
Scatter me with the breeze in your hands then gather me up
The night renders up its soul to you Intruder
and a star can't see me without knowing how my family
    will kill me with rosewater
So give me the sudden happiness that needs me
and I will break my jar with my own hands

You suggest I change my path?
I didn't say anything – my life is beyond me
I'm the me saying:
The last poem fell from my date palms
I travel within myself
besieged by contradictions
And life is worth the candle of its mystery
and its prophetic birds

I wasn't born to know I was going to die
but to love what's in God's shadow

Beauty takes me to the beautiful
And I love your love
freed from itself and its signs

I am my alternative
I am the one who says to himself:
From the smallest things are born the largest thoughts
Rhythm doesn't come from the words
but from the joining of two bodies in a long night . . .

I'm the one talking to himself to tame memory . . . are you
    me?
You, me and the third which is the two of us
fluttering between and declaring, don't forget!
O our death! Take us then
so we can learn to shine . . .
On me there's no sun or moon
I left my gloom hanging on a branch of a boxthorn
and the place weighed less
As my fugitive spirit took to the sky

I'm the me saying:
O girl what did the longed-for ones do to you?
The breeze ruffles and carries us like autumn scents
My woman you grew on my crutches
And now they'll speed you on your way
sure-sighted to Damascus
A guardian angel and two doves fly over what's left of our
    lives
And the land is a festival . . .

The land is a festival of the vanquished and we are among them
It's we who brought the anthem here
camping in the wind like an old eagle's feather
We were good and pious without Christ's teachings
and stronger than the grass at summer's end
You are my truth and I your question
We have inherited nothing but our names
And you are my playground and I your shade
at the crossroads of the anthem

We weren't there when the saints and their magic and
     malice got into the anthem
On the horns of a mountain goat they carried the place
     from its time to another time
It would have been more natural if the stars in our sky
     were a fraction higher than the stones in our well
and the prophets less nagging
Then the soldiers could have heard our praises

Green
The land of my poem is green
The song carries her as she was
fertile from past to past
And I have of her: Narcissus contemplating the water of
     his image
And I have of her: the sharpness of shadows in synonyms
     and the exactitude of meaning . . .
And I have of her: what is common in the sayings of
     prophets on the roof of the night

And I have of her: the donkey of wisdom abandoned on a
    hill, mocking her legends and her reality . . .
And I have of her: the symbols stuffed with opposites
Realism doesn't find memories
Abstraction doesn't lead to illumination
My other self I have of her
Singers can only inscribe her days in a diary:
If the dream isn't enough
I'll be heroically sleepless at the door of exile
And I have of her: the echo of my language from the walls
removing salt from the sea
at the very moment when my strong heart betrays me

Higher than the valley was my wisdom
When I told the devil: No, don't test me!
Don't give me your either-ors
Leave me in the Old Testament climbing to heaven
there is my kingdom
Take hold of history O son of my father
take history and make with guesses what you need

And I have tranquillity
A small grain of wheat will be enough for us
for me and my brother the enemy
Since my hour hasn't yet come
nor the hour of the harvest
I must embrace absence, listen to my heart and follow it
to Kana in Galilee
My hour has not yet come
Perhaps something in myself rejects me

Perhaps I am someone else
The figs are not yet ripe around the girls' dresses
and from the feather of the ostrich I have not yet been born
Nobody is waiting for me there
I have come before and I have come after
I find nobody who believes what I see
I the one who sees
am far away
The faraway

My me who are you?
We are two on the road
and one at the resurrection
Take me to the light of my disappearance to see how I'll
    be in my other mirror
Who my me will I be after you?
Is my body behind me or before you?
Who am I you tell me?
Make me as I make you
anoint me with almond oil
crown me with cedar
and transport me from the valley to a white eternity
Teach me life on the way
test me like an atom in the heavens
come to my aid against the boredom of the eternal
and be lenient when the roses pierce from my veins and
    wound me . . .

Our hour has not yet come
No prophet counts time with a fistful of late grass

Has time closed its circle?
No angels visit the place so poets can leave their past
    behind on the dusk's horizon
and open by hand their tomorrows
Sing again Anat darling goddess
my first poem about genesis
Storytellers have already found the willow's
birth certificate in the autumn stone
and shepherds their well in the depth of a song
And time has already come for those who play with
    meaning
on a butterfly's wing caught in rhymes

So sing darling goddess
I am both the prey Anat and the arrows
I am words
the funeral oration the call of the muezzin
and the martyr

I haven't said goodbye to the ruins yet
So don't be what I was except once
once was enough to see how time collapses itself like a
    bedouin tent
in a wind from the north
How places split apart and the what-has-gone wears the
    litter of a deserted temple
Everything around me looks like me
and I look like nothing here
As if the earth is too small for the lyrically sick

descendents of the poor crazy devils who when they had a
   good dream
taught love poetry to a parrot
and saw all frontiers open ...

I want to live ...
I have work to do on deck
not to save birds from our famines or sea sickness
but to study the deluge close-up
And after?
What do survivors do with the ancient land?
Do they take up the same story?
How did it begin?
What's the epilogue?
No one comes back from death to tell us the truth ...

Wait for me Death beyond the earth
Wait for me on your land
until I finish my talk with what's left of my life
not far from your tent
Wait for me til I finish reading Tarafa bin al Abed

The existentialists who drew up from the well of each moment
freedom
justice
the wine of the gods ...
They seduce me

So wait Death til I have settled the funeral arrangements
   in the clear spring of my birth

and have forbidden the orators to lyricise again
about the sad land and the steadfastness of figs and olives
   in the face of time's armies
Dissolve me I'd say in all the femininity of the letter
   "nuun"[1]
Let me gulp down the Sura of the Merciful in the Qur'an
And walk with me in my ancestors' footsteps
silently to the rhythm of a flute
towards my eternity
And don't place a violet on my grave
it's the flower of the depressed
and reminds the dead of how love died too young
Place seven ears of green wheat on my coffin and a few
   red anemones should you find them
otherwise leave the church roses for churches and newly-
   weds

Wait til I pack my bag Death
my toothbrush soap after-shave and some clothes
Is the climate warm over there?
Do the seasons change in the eternal whiteness?
Or does the weather stay fixed in autumn or winter?
Will one book be enough to read in non-time?
Or should I take a library?
And what do they talk over there?
vernacular or classical?

Death wait for me Death
til I clear my mind in Spring
and regain my health

Then you'll be the noble hunter who doesn't kill the
    gazelle while it's drinking

Let's be friendly and open together
I'll give you my well-filled life
and you give me a view of the planets
No one exactly dies
Rather souls change their looks and address
Death my shadow who will lead me
You the third in two
You hesitant colour of sapphires and topaz
You blood of the peacock
You poacher of a fox's heart
You, our delirium!
Sit
Put down your hunting things outside under the awning
Hang your set of heavy keys above the door!
You Mighty One stop looking at my veins monitoring the
    last drop
You are mightier than medicine
mightier than the respirator
mightier than pungent honey
You don't need to kill me – my sickness will
Why not be nobler than the insects?
Be transparently yourself
a visible message to be read by the invisible
Be like love – a storm among trees
Don't stand on the threshold like a beggar or tax collector
Don't be an undercover policeman directing traffic
Be strong like shining steel and take off the fox's mask

Be chivalrous glamorous fatal
Say what you want to say:
I come from one meaning and go to another
Life is liquid
and I thicken it and define it
with my pair of scales and sceptre
Death wait
take a seat
drink a glass of wine
and don't bargain with me
Someone like you doesn't bargain with anyone
and someone like me doesn't argue with the herald of the
    invisible

Take it easy – perhaps you're worn out by star wars
Who am I that you should visit me?
Have you time to check out my poem?
No that's not your concern
your concern is with the clay of man's being
not with what he does or says
You're defeated Death by the arts by each one of them
You're defeated by the songs of the land of two rivers
By the Egyptian obelisk by the tomb of the Pharaohs
In the temples there are bas-reliefs who defeated you
And eternity escaped through your cracks
So carry on with yourself
and with us
as you see fit

And I want
I want to live
I have work to do on the geography of volcanoes
From desolation to ruin
from the time of Lott to Hiroshima
As if I'd never yet lived
with a lust I've still to know
Perhaps Now has gone further away
and yesterday come closer
So I take Now's hand to walk along the hem of history
and avoid cyclic time
with its chaos of mountain goats
How can my tomorrow be saved?
By the velocity of electronic time
or by my desert caravan slowness?
I have work til my end
as if I won't see tomorrow
and I have work for today who isn't here
So I listen
softly softly
to the ant beat of my heart. Bear with me my patience
I hear the cry of the imprisoned stone: let me go
In a violin I see yearning's migration between peat and
    sky
And in my feminine hand
I hold tight my familiar eternity:
I was created then loved then died then awoke on the
    grass of my tombstone
whose letters from time to time refer to me
What's the use of Spring if it doesn't please the dead

and show them the joy of life and the shock of
    forgetfulness?
That's the clue to my poems
at least the sentimental ones
And what on earth are dreams if not our only way of
    speaking?

Take your time Death
Take a seat on the crystal of my days
as if you've always been a constant friend
as if you were the foreigner among living creatures
You are the exile
You haven't a life
Your life is only my death
You neither live nor die
You kidnap children between their thirst for milk and
    milk
You'll never be a child in a cradle rocked by finches
never will angels and stags tease you with their horns
as they teased us
we guests of the butterfly
You are the miserable exile
with no woman pressing you to her breasts
no woman to make during the long night
nostalgia Two
in the language of desire
and to make into One
the land and heaven which is in us
No boy of yours to say: Father I love you
You are the exile

You king of kings
There's no praise for your sceptre
no falcon waiting on your horse
no pearls embedded in your crown
You are stripped of flags and music
How can you go around like a cowardly thief without
    guards or singers?
Who do you think you are?
You're the Great Highness of Death
Mighty leader of the invincible Assyrians

So do with us
and yourself
as you see fit

And I want I want to live to forget you
and dismiss our long affair as nothing
So I can read the letters written by the faraway sky
Each time I readied myself you failed to show up
Each time I said Wait! so I may finish the last lap of two
    bodies becoming one
You said mockingly: Don't forget we have an appointment
When is it?
Is it at oblivion's summit
Where the world gives up and bows down to the temple's
    wood and the animals painted in caves?
Saying: I'm nothing but what I leave behind
and my only son
Where is our appointment?
Permit me to select a café by the door of the sea?

No
Don't come to God's shore, you son of sinners, son of
    Adam
you were born to labour not question

Be amicable yes you Death amicable
become abstract so I can grasp the essence of your
    unfindable wisdom!
Perhaps you taught Cain to throw too soon?
Perhaps you should have taught Job more patience?
Perhaps you saddled your horse Death to take me on my
    horse?
As if when I confront forgetfulness my language saves me
As if I'm eternally present eternally flying
As if since knowing you my drugged tongue has become
    addicted to your white chariot
higher than the clouds of sleep
higher than when the senses are freed from the burden of
    matter
Yet you and I on the road to God are like two Sufis
    following a vision
both of us blind

Retreat under protection and by yourself Death
For I am free in this here of neither here nor there
retreat to your lonely exile
Fetch your hunting gear
and wait for me by the door of the sea
Prepare some red wine for my return to the clinic in the
    land of the sick

Don't be crude O sledgehammer of hearts!
I didn't come to mock you nor to walk on water in the
    soul's north
But still
you led me astray
and I neglected the end of my poem:
I didn't carry my mother on my mare to marry my father
I left the door ajar for an Andalusia of songs
and sat myself on a fence of almonds and pomegranates
brushing out cobwebs from my grandfathers' grandfathers'
    clothes
whilst foreign armies pass by along the ancient road
punctuating time with the same ancient war machine

Death is this history your twin or your ravine opposite?
The dove builds her nest in an iron helmet
And wormwood may sprout from the wheels of a
    destroyed chariot
What does History your twin or opposite do to nature
    when earth meets heaven and the holy rain rains?

Death
wait for me
at the door to the sea in the café of romantics
Don't come back until your arrow misses one last time
Like this I can say farewell to my inside from my outside
Like this I can proffer my wheat-filled soul to blackbirds
    perched on my hand and shoulder
Like this I can say goodbye to the land that drinks my salt
    and sows me as pasture for the horses and gazelles

Wait whilst I finish my short visit to time and place
Don't argue about whether or not I'm coming back
I'm going to thank life
while neither living nor dead
Death the supreme one you're the orphan!

My nurse tells me: you were shivering violently and
     screaming: O heart!
O heart take me to the toilet . . .
What's the use of my soul if my body's sick and can't
     evacuate?
O Heart Heart bring back my footsteps so I can go to the
     toilet alone!
I've forgotten my arms legs two knees
and how gravity works with an apple
and how the heart functions
I've forgotten Eve's garden at the entry to eternity
I've forgotten the use of my small organs
I've forgotten how to breathe with my lungs
I've forgotten speech
I'm scared for my language
Leave the rest and just bring back my language!

My nurse says: you were shivering violently and screaming:
I don't want to return to anyone
I don't want to return to any land
After this long absence
I want only to return to my language deep in the cooing
     of a dove
My nurse says you kept shivering and asking me:

Is death what you're doing with me right now?
Or is this how language dies?

Green the land of my poem is green and high
Slowly I tell it slowly with the grace of a seagull riding
    the waves on the book of water
I bequeath it written down to the one who asks: to whom
    shall we sing when salt poisons the dew?
Green I write it on prose of wheat in the book of fields
stalks bending with our weight
Whenever I befriended or became a brother to an ear of wheat
annihilation and its opposite taught me survival
I am the grain that died and became green again
there is something of life in death

I suppose I am I suppose I'm not
No one died instead of me
Thanks apart what words do the dead remember:
God have mercy on our souls
I enjoy recalling verses I've forgotten
I didn't engender a son to bear the burden of his father's
    death
I prefer the open marriage of words
the feminine stumbling on the masculine
in the ebb of poetry towards prose
A sycamore will take my limbs as branches
and my heart will pour its muddy water into a planet
Who will I be in death after myself?
Who was I in death before myself?
A spectre proclaimed

Osiris was like us
and the son of Mary was like you
and like me
an agony convulses a dying nothingness
promising that death is temporary
a trick . . .

Frome where does poetry come?
From the heart's intelligence
from a hunch about the unknown
or from a rose in the desert?
The personal is not personal
and the universal not universal

I suppose I am I suppose I'm not
The more I listen to my heart the more I'm filled with the
    words of the unseen
and lifted high to the treetops
I fly aimless from dream to dream
Belonging to a thousand years of poetry
born in the darkness of white linen
I don't know who amongst us was I
and who the dream
Am I my dream?

I suppose I am I suppose I'm not
My language doesn't lose its ruminant lilt til it migrates
    north
Our dogs quietened
our goats in the hills lost in mist

a stray arrow lodges in the face of certitude
my language on horseback wearies me quibbling about
    what the past makes of the days of Imru al Qays
who was caught between poetry and Caesar

Each time I turn my face to the gods
there in the land of lavender
I'm lit by Anat's round moon
Anat the mistress so the story goes of metaphor
She mourns no one
but weeps for her own attractions:
Is this magic my own
or is it offered me by the poet
who shared the emptiness of my bed of glory?
and plucked abundant flowers
from the thicket of my playfulness
Or by that poet who coaxed night's milk in my breast?
I'm the beginning
I'm the ending
And my limits outdo my limits
And my harts run after me in words
nothing before and nothing after

I won't dream of repairing
the axle of the wind's chariot
or of healing the wounds of the soul
Myths are traps along the course of the real
and in the poem there's no room to alter the passing of the
    past that won't pass
or to stop the earthquake

I will dream in the hope that countries expand to make
    room for me as I am
an orphan cut off from the people of this sea

Stop asking me hard questions
Who am I you ask
am I my mother's son?
I don't doubt much
I can do without shepherds and kings
My today like my tomorrow is with me
I have with me a small notebook
and each time a cloud grazes a bird I write: a dream has
    freed my wings
and I am flying too
Everything that is alive flies
And I am me
nothing more

I'm one of the people of this plain
When the feast-day for barley arrives
I'll visit my magnificent remains
they're a tattoo
the winds can't preserve or scatter
And when the feast day for vineyards arrives
Drink for me a glass of wine from a peddler
My soul is light
My body heavy with memory and places
In spring I'll become a tourist's impressions scrawled on a
    postcard:

On the left of the deserted stage a lily and a walking
    shadow
on the right a modern city

And I am me
nothing more
I'm not a Roman legion guarding the salt roads
I pay a toll for the salt in my bread
and I say to history:
Decorate your lorries with lowly slaves and lowly kings
and you will pass . . .
No one henceforth will say No

And I am me
nothing more
I belong to the people of this night
and I dream on my horse going up and up
following the river to its source behind the mountain

Listen Horse be sure-footed
for in the wind we can't be told apart
You are my youth and I'm your shadow
Stand firm like Aleph and strike lightening
Search with your hoof for the pulsating desire there in the echo
Stand tall like Aleph
Hold firm and be erect as Aleph
Don't fall on the last foothill like an abandoned ensign in
    the alphabet
In the wind we can't be told apart

You are my cover I'm your metaphor
To hell with tame processions
Faster Horse!
Pull my past into a place that is mine
for place is the path and there's no path save you
shod as you are with the winds
Make sparks in the mirage!
Show me clouds in the nothingness
be guide and brother to my light
Don't die before me or after me on the last foothill
Don't die with me
Warn me of the ambulance
and the dead
I may – who knows – still be alive

I will dream
Not to change the apparent result
but to rescue myself from the dry penury of my soul
I remember by heart all my heart
who is no longer a fretful child
one aspirin calms and mollifies him
my neighbouring heart has become a stranger
and I'm no longer at the beck of his wishes
or of his women

The heart rusts like iron
It no longer takes
no longer gives
no longer feels the first rain of desire
no more laments like the dry August grass

my heart is turned into a hermit
similes no longer speak
When the heart dries up
aesthetics become geometric
feelings wear cloaks
and virginity becomes cunning

Each time I turned to face the first songs
there were tracks of a sand grouse on the words
I wasn't the child who happily said: yesterday was
    better
But memory's two light hands can rock and make the
    earth tremble
and in an exile's veins memory can carry the weeping
    scent of night flowers
which make him declare:
Be my grief's ascent then I'll find my time . . .
Then all I'll need
to follow the ancient ships
will be one beat of a seagull's wing

How long ago did we discover Time and Death
the synonymous twins of life?
Maybe we're still alive because death forgot us?
We with our gift of memory are free
to walk the green walk of Gilgamesh
from age to age

Being is a perfect speck of dust . . .
Absence shatters me as if I were a small jug of water

Enkidu went to sleep and didn't wake up
And my wings slept swaddled in a handful of their own
    clay feathers
The gods are wind turned to stone
My left arm a wooden stick
My heart is abandoned like a dry well
and the savage echo shouts: Enkidu!

My imagination will give out before I finish the journey
I don't have the energy to make my dream real
Give me my weapons so I can polish them with the salt of
    tears
Give me tears Enkidu
So the dead in us may weep for the living
And me?
Who has gone to sleep now Enkidu?
Is it me or you?

Our Gods are a fistful of wind
So wake me with all the fickleness of your humanity
And let's dream that in some slight way the gods and us
    are equal
We who restore the beautiful land between the Tigris and
    Euphrates and cherish its names

Friend how have I bored you?
And you've left me
Without youth's zeal wisdom is useless
You killed me my friend when you left me at the door of
    the labyrinth

Now it's up to me alone to watch over our fate
and like a love-furious bull carry the world on my
     shoulders
I have to find alone an exit from the footsteps of my destiny
I have to solve the riddle Enkidu

Myself my will and my strength are yours
I will carry your life to your place
So who am I alone
surrounded by Being's perfect nothingness?
Notwithstanding
I lean your naked shadow against a date palm
But where is your shadow?
After your trunk broke where is your shadow?
Man's summit
is his
abyss

I was unfair when I confronted the beast in you
with a woman's milk
Quenching you I tamed you . . .
and you surrendered to my humanity.
Enkidu be a friend and return to where you died
perhaps there we'll find the answer
For who am I alone?
A lone life is missing something
and I'm missing the question
Who can I ask about the river's passing?
So wake up my brother of salt
Carry me

When you're sleeping do you notice?
Wake up
You're sleeping!
Move before the wise men surround me like jackals
All is vanity
so seize your life as it is
an instant full of the demands of rising sap
Live for this day not for your dream
everything is ephemeral
Beware of tomorrow and live today in a woman who loves
    you
live for your body not your illusion
And wait
A child will carry your soul in your place
immortality is procreation nothing less
everything is vain or ephemeral
ephemeral or vain

Who am I?
The Song of Songs?
or the wisdom of Ecclesiastics?
You and I are me
I'm poet
and king
and a wise man at the edge of the well
No cloud in my open hand
in my temple no eleven planets
my body narrow
my eternity narrow
and my tomorrow sitting like a crown of dust on my throne

Vain vanity of vanities . . . vain
Everything on earth is ephemeral
The winds are north
the winds are south
The sun rises by itself and sets by itself
nothing is new
The past was yesterday
futile in futility
The temple is high
and the wheat is high
If the sky comes down it rains
and if the land rises up it's destroyed
Anything that goes beyond its limits will become its
    opposite one day
And life on earth is a shadow of something we can't see

Vain vanity of vanities . . . vain
Everything on earth is ephemeral
1,400 chariots
12,000 horses
Carry my gilded name from one age to another
I lived as no other poet
a king and sage
I grew old and bored with glory
I didn't lack for anything
Is this why the more my star rose the more my anxiety
    grew?
So what's Jerusalem and what's a throne
if nothing remains forever?

There's a time for birth
and a time for death
A time for silence
and a time for speech
A time for war
and a time for peace
and a time for time
nothing remains forever
Each river will be drunk by the sea
and the sea still is not full
Nothing remains forever
everything living will die
and death is still not full
Nothing will remain after me except a gilded name:
"Solomon was . . ."
So what do the dead do with their names?
Is it the gold
or the song of songs
or the Ecclesiastes
who will illuminate the vastness of my gloom?

Vain vanity of vanities . . . vain
everything on earth is ephemeral
I saw myself walking like Christ on the lake
but I came down from the cross because of my fear of
    heights
and I don't preach the resurrection
All that I changed was my pace the better to hear the
    voice of my heart

Eagles are for bards
for me the dove's collar
a star abandoned above the roof
and a winding alley in Akka leading to the port
nothing more or less
I want to say good morning there to the happy boy I was
Happy child I was not
But distance is a brilliant blacksmith who can forge a
    moon from worthless scrap

You know me?
I ask a shadow against the walls
A young girl wearing fire takes note and says:
You speaking to me?
No, I reply, I'm speaking to my double
Another Majnun Layla inspecting ruins, she mutters
and disappears into her shop at the end of the suq

It was here
we were
two date palms
relaying to the sea the messages of certain poets
Neither me nor I have grown up much
The seascape the ramparts defending our defeat
the hint of incense
announce we are still here
even if time has gone from the place
we can never be separated

So you know me? shouts the me I left
We can't be split and we have never met
Then he ties two small waves to his arms and soars high
into the sky
and I ask: which of us migrated?

I asked a jailer on the western shore: are you the son of
my old jailer?
Yes indeed
Where's your father?
He replied: Father died years ago laid low with the
boredom of guarding
He left me his profession and told me to guard the town
against your songs
I said: how long have you been surveying me and
imprisoning yourself?
He replied: since you wrote your first one
I said: but you weren't born yet!
He said: I have time and eternity I want to live to the
rhythm of America within the walls of Jerusalem
I said: whoever you are – I'm leaving
and the me you see now isn't me I'm just a ghost
He said: you're an echo in a stone nothing more
that's why you never left or stayed
that's why you're still in your yellowed cell
so let me get on with my work!
I said: am I still here freed or captured without knowing it?
Is the sea behind the walls my sea?
He said: you're a prisoner, prisoner of yourself and
nostalgia!

The me you see isn't me – I am my ghost
So I say speaking to myself: I am alive
and I ask: If two ghosts meet in the desert do they share
    the sand
or fight for monopoly of the night?

The clock in the port ticks on
No one notices its time at night
The fishermen of the generous sea cast their nets and plait
    the waves
the lovers are in the discotheque
Dreamers caress sleeping larks
and dream
I said: If I died I would wake up
I have more than enough of the past
but not enough of tomorrow ...

I will walk in my footsteps down the old path through the
    sea air
no woman will see me passing under her balcony
I have of memories only those necessary for the long
    journey
Days contain all they need of tomorrows
I was smaller than my eyelashes and my two dimples
So take my sleepiness
and hide me in the story of the tender evening
Hide me under one of the two date palms
and teach me poetry
So I can learn how to walk beside Homer
So I can add to the story a description of Akka

the oldest of the beautiful cities
the most beautiful of the old cities
A box of stone
where the living and dead move in the dry clay
like bees captive in a honeycomb in a hive
and each time the siege tightens
they go on a flower hunger strike
and ask the sea to indicate the emergency exit

Teach me poetry
in case a girl needs a song
for her distant beloved:
Take me to you even by force and prepare my bed in
    your hands
And they walked interlaced towards the echo
as though I had married a runaway fawn to a gazelle
and opened the church door for the pigeons

Teach me poetry
She who spun the wool shirt
and waits by the door
is first to speak of the horizon and despair:
The fighter hasn't returned and won't return
and you are not the you I was waiting for

I saw myself like Christ on the lake . . .
But I came down from the cross because of my fear of heights
and I don't preach the apocalypse
all that I changed was my pace the better to hear the voice
    of my heart . . .

Eagles are for bards
for me
the dove's collar
a star abandoned on the roof
and a winding alley leading to the port
This sea is mine
This sea air is mine
This quayside with my footsteps and sperm upon it . . . is
    mine
And the old bus station is mine
And my ghost and its master are mine
And the copper utensils and the verse of the throne
and the key are mine
And the door and the guards and bells are mine
The horseshoe flung over the ramparts is mine
All that was mine is mine
Paper scraps torn from the gospels are mine
Salt from the tears on the wall of the house are mine . . .
And my name mispronounced with its five horizontal letters
my name . . . is mine:

mim/ of lovesickness of the orphan of those who
    complete the past
ha/ of the garden and love, of two muddles and two losses
mim/ of the rake of the lovesick of the exile prepared for
    a death foretold
waw/ of farewells of the central flower of fidelity to birth
    wherever it may be and of a parent's promise
dal/ of the guide of the path of tears of a studied galaxy
    and a sparrow who cajoles me and makes me bleed

This name is mine . . .
and also my friends' wherever they may be
And my temporary body is mine
present or absent . . .
Two metres of this earth will be enough for now
a metre and 75 centimetres for me
and the rest for flowers in a riot of colour
who will slowly drink me
And what was mine is mine: my yesterday
and what will be in the distant tomorrow in the return of
    the fugitive soul
as if nothing has been
and as if nothing has been
A light wound on the arm of the absurd present
History taunting its victims
and its heroes . . .
throwing them a glance and passing on
This sea is mine
This sea air is mine
And my name – if I mispronounce it on my coffin – is
    mine
And as for me – full of all reasons for leaving –
I am not mine
I am not mine
I am not mine

The Dice Player

Who am I to say to you
what I'm saying?

I wasn't a stone washed by water
so I became a face
I wasn't a reed pierced by the wind
so I became a flute

I'm the way the dice fall
sometimes winning sometimes losing
I'm like you
or maybe slightly less . . .

I was born beside the well
where three single trees stood like nuns
I was born without ceremony or a midwife
and belonged to a family
by chance
inheriting its features, idiosyncrasies
and illnesses:

First: feeble arteries and high blood pressure
Second: shyness in talking with mother, father,
    grandmother – or a tree
Third: the belief that flu can be cured with a hot cup of
    chamomile
Fourth: a disinclination to talk about gazelles or skylarks
Fifth: a tendency to boredom on winter nights
Sixth: a farcical inability to sing

I had no say in who I was
It was by chance I turned out
male
by chance that I found the upturned moon
pale as a lemon
urging on the night

and just as easily
could find a mole hidden in the deepest recess of my
    groin

It's possible
I might not have been
and my father might not have been
then he wouldn't have married my mother
by chance
I might have been like my sister
who screamed then died and never knew it
because she lived for an hour and didn't know her
    mother . . .

Or one could say: like a pigeon's egg which breaks before
    the chick can hatch from its shell

I happened by chance
me the survivor of the bus accident
because I was late going to school
forgetting the here and now
while reading a love story at night
losing myself in story-teller and victim of love
til I became a martyr of passion in the story
and the survivor of the bus accident!

I can't see myself joking with the sea
but I am a reckless kid
one of my hobbies is to dawdle in the waves
when they're singing: Come to me!
And I can't see myself being rescued from the sea
I was saved by a sort of seagull
who saw the playful waves paralyzing my hand

It's possible
I wouldn't have been struck with the madness of the *Jahili*
    *Mu'alaqaat*²
if the door of the house had faced North
and not overlooked the sea
if the army patrol hadn't seen the fire of the villagers
    making bread that night
if 15 martyrs had been able to rebuild the barricades
if that rural place hadn't been obliterated

perhaps I'd have become an olive tree
or a geography teacher
or an expert in the realm of ants
or guardian of an echo!

who am I to say to you
what I'm saying
at the door of the church
I'm nothing but the fall of the dice
landing between predator and prey
winning a clarity that obscures my happiness on moonlit
    nights
and obliges me to witness the carnage

It was by chance
I escaped
I was smaller than a military target
and larger than a bee hovering between the flowers on the
    fence
I feared a lot for my brothers and father
feared for time made of glass
feared for my cat and my rabbit
feared for the magical moon above the high minaret of the
    mosque
feared for the grapes on the vine dangling like the teats of
    our dog
Fear walked in me and I walked in it
barefoot
forgetting my little memories or what I want from
    tomorrow

– there's no time for tomorrow –
I walk, scramble, run, climb, get down, scream, bark,
   howl, call out, wail, speed up, slow down, love, become
   lighter, drier, march on, fly, see, don't see, stumble,
   become yellow, green, blue, gasp, sob, thirst, get
   tired, struggle, fall, get up, run, forget, see, don't see,
   remember, hear, look, wonder, hallucinate, mumble,
   yell I can't, moan, go mad, stay, become less and more,
   fall, rise, collapse, bleed and faint

And by chance
with my lack of luck
the wolves disappeared from there
or we escaped the soldiers

I have no say in my life
except that I am
when life taught me its hymns
I said: do you have more?
so I lit its lantern
and it tried to oblige

I might not have been a swallow
if the wind had wanted it that way
the wind is the luck of the traveler
I went north, east and west
but the south was far and impenetrable to me
because the south is my home
So I became a metaphor of a swallow soaring above my
   debris

in Spring and Autumn
trying out my feathers in the clouds above the lake
scattering my greetings on my protector
who does not die
because he has God's soul
and God is the luck of the prophet

Luckily I live next to the divinities
Unluckily
the cross is the only ladder to our tomorrow

Who am I to say to you
what I'm saying
Who am I?

It's possible
inspiration might not have come
inspiration is the luck of the loner
this poem is a dice throw
onto a board of darkness
that glows and doesn't glow
words fall
like feathers on sand

I don't think it was me who wrote the poem
I just obeyed its rhythm:
the flow of feelings each affecting the next
meaning given by intuition
a trance in the echoing words
the image of myself taken from me and given to another

with no one to help me
and my longing for the source

I don't think it was me who wrote the poem
except when inspiration stopped
and inspiration is the luck of the skillful
when they apply themselves

The only possibility was
to love the girl who asked me:
What time is it?
on my way to the cinema.
And it was only possible for her to be a mulatta
which she was
or a passing mystery and a darkness

It's like this the words multiply
I induce my heart to love so it has room for flowers and
        thorns ...
My vocabulary is mystic and my desires corporeal
And I'm not who I am now unless there's a meeting of
        two:
me and my feminine self

Love! What are you?
How much are you? You
and not you?
Love! Rage like a tempest over us
so we can find only what the divinities want of my body
and pour away the rest in a funnel

You – whether displayed or hidden –
have no shape
and we love you when we love
by chance
You're the luck of the poor

Unfortunately
I often escaped love's closure
but fortunately stayed fit enough to re-open its door!

Secretly, the canny lover says to himself:
Love is our truthful lie
Overhearing him, his beloved replies:
love comes and goes
like lightening and thunder

To life I say: slow down wait for me until intoxication has
     dried out in my glass
In the garden all the flowers are ours
and the wind can't unwind itself from the rose
Wait for me so the nightingales don't flee the town square
and make me break the rhythm
while the minstrels tighten their strings for the goodbye
     song
Go slow for me and be brief so the song won't take long
lest my delivery interrupt the prelude and split it in two
let two and two make one
Long Live Life!
Take your time and take me in your arms
so the wind doesn't scatter me

Even when I'm carried by the wind
I can't unwind myself from the alphabet

If I hadn't scaled the mountain
I might have been happy with an eagle's eyrie: nothing
    loftier
but such glory crowned with infinite blue gold
is difficult to visit:
Up there the loner stays lonely
and can't come down on his feet
So no eagle walks
no human flies
How much a peak resembles an abyss
You - o solitude of the summit know it!

I have no say in what I was
or will be . . .
It's luck.
And luck has no name
We might name it:
the blacksmith of our fate or
the postman of the heavens or
the carpenter of the newborn's cradle and the dead man's
    coffin or
Let's call it the legendary gods' servant
whose lines we wrote while hiding behind Olympus . . .
which the hungry potters believed
but the bloated lords of gold didn't
unluckily for their author
this ghost standing on the stage is real

Behind the scenes it's something else
the question is no longer: When?
but: Why? How? And Who?

Who am I to say to you
what I'm saying?

It's possible not to have been
suppose the convoy fell into an ambush
and suppose the family lost a son
like the one now writing this poem
letter by letter
bleeding and bleeding
on this sofa
blood black as black
not a crow's ink
nor its caw
it's the whole night squeezed out by hand
drop by drop
by the hand of luck and talent

It's possible that poetry might have gained more
if precisely this poet hadn't existed
a hoopoe at the edge of the abyss
Though the poet might say: If I'd been another
I would become only me again

This is how I bluff:
Narcissus wasn't as beautiful as he thought.
His creators trapped him in his reflection

so I ripple the smooth image with droplets of water . . .
Suppose he'd been able to see someone other than himself
and could have seen the love of a girl gazing at him
forget the stags running between the lilies and daisies . . .
if he'd been just a fraction cleverer
he'd have smashed the mirror
and seen how much he was like to others
Yet if he'd been free
he wouldn't have become a myth . . .

In the desert the mirage is the traveler's book
and without it
without the mirage
he won't continue searching for water
There's a cloud, he tells himself carrying his jug of hope
    in one hand and clutching his belly with the other
and he thumbs his errors into the sand
to corral the clouds into a pit
And the mirage calls him, lures, misleads him
then lifts him up:
read if you can't read
write if you can't write
So he reads: water water water
and writes a sentence in the sand:
without the mirage I wouldn't be alive til now

And it's the luck of the traveler that
hope is the twin of despair
or else his improvised poetry

When the sky is grey
and I see a rose sprouting through the cracks in a wall
I don't say: the sky is grey
but keep my eye on the rose and tell it:
it's quite a day!

Just as at nightfall
I say to my two friends:
If there has to be a dream
let it be like us and simple
For example: after two days
the three of us will dine
to fete our dream's premonition
that after two days
not one of us will have been lost
So let's celebrate in the moon's sonata
and make a toast to the lenience of death
who saw the three of us happy together
and decided to look the other way!

I don't say: far away life is real with its imaginary places
I say: life here is possible

By chance this land became holy
its lakes hills and trees aren't replicas of those in paradise
It became holy because a prophet walked here
prayed on a rock that began to weep
and the mount fell down from fear of God
then passed out

And by chance the slope of a field in this country
becomes a museum of dust
because too many soldiers from both sides die there
defending two leaders
who waiting in two silken tents for their spoils
give the order to Charge!
Soldiers die time and again without ever knowing who
    won

Meanwhile the surviving storytellers say:
if by chance the others had won!
History's headlines could have been different

O land I love you green
Green
an apple dancing in water and light
Green
your night green, your dawn green
so plant me with the tenderness of a mother's hand
in a handful of air
I am one of your seeds
Green . . .

That stanza has more than one poet
and it's possible it didn't have to be lyrical

Who am I to say to you
what I'm saying?
It would have been possible not to be who I am
It would have been possible not to be here . . .

it would have been possible
if the plane had crashed that morning with me on board
Luckily I'm a late riser
and missed the flight

It would have been possible never to have visited Cairo
   Damascus the Louvre and other magical cities
If I'd been walking slower
the rifle shot might have cut my shadow off from
the watchful cypress

If I'd been walking faster
I might have been shattered to pieces by shrapnel
and become a passing thought

It's possible if I'd dreamed more excessively
I might have lost my memory

Luckily I sleep alone
and listen carefully to my body
and believe in my gift for discerning pain
in time to call the doctor
ten minutes before dying
Ten minutes is enough for me to live by chance
and to defy nothingness

Who am I to defy nothingness?
who am I? who am I?

Notes

1. *Nūn*. Letter of the Arabic alphabet similar to the letter N. It is known as *Nun al-Nisswa* (the feminizing N) as it is used as a suffix indicating plural feminine nouns in the present tense. In contrast to the norm of most Arabic dialects, the colloquial dialect of Darwish's western Galilee uses the feminine suffix *hun* instead of the masculine *hum* for both masculine and feminine objects in the plural.
2. *Jahili Mu'allaqaat*. Pre-Islamic "hanging poems." These were the seven greatest poems of the pre-Islamic era that, according to (later) medieval literary lore, were given the honour of being hung from the walls of the *Ka'aba* in Mecca.

How am I born from a thing I later make?

I extend in the high trees
to heaven, I become a cautious bird
that nothing deceives or obliterates
deceives

and the thing raises me

In each thing I see my soul and what I cannot feel hurts me.
And what doesn't feel the hurt that cannot it
also
hurts
me

Make me as I make you
anoint me with almond oil
crown me with cedar
and transport me from the valley to a
white eternity

My me who are you?
We are two on the road
and one at the resurrection

Take me to the light of my disappearance
to see how I'll be in my other mirror

Who will be my me after you?
        Is my body behind me or after you   ?
Who am I to tell you?

I made these drawings during the days immediately following the news of Mahmoud Darwish's untimely death on 9 August 2008. Whilst living with and translating over many, many months the two long poems that constitute this book, we had grown accustomed to imagining his speaking voice and anticipating hearing it again.

He writes in the poems about those he loves and about himself whilst continually bantering with Death. Nevertheless we were unprepared for his voice no longer being audible – except on CDs. The drawings were made in an attempt to fill such an abrupt silence.

And then something happened, for Mahmoud's written lines began, like rhizome plants, to intermingle and entwine with the drawn lines, and this was a kind of reply.